Anthony

Rea

Methuen Drama

Published by Methuen Drama 2011

Methuen Drama, an imprint of Bloomsbury Publishing Plc

1 3 5 7 9 10 8 6 4 2

Methuen Drama
Bloomsbury Publishing Plc
36 Soho Square
London W1D 3QY
www.methuendrama.com

ISBN: 978 1 408 15718 3

Available in the USA from Bloomsbury Academic & Professional,
175 Fifth Avenue/3rd Floor, New York, NY 10010.
www.BloomsburyAcademicUSA.com

A CIP catalogue record for this book is available from the British Library

Typeset by Country Setting, Kingsdown, Kent
Printed and bound in Great Britain by
CPI Antony Rowe, Chippenham and Eastbourne

Soho Theatre presents

Anthony Neilson's REALISM

Realism was first presented at the Royal Lyceum Theatre, Edinburgh in August 2006. It had its English premiere at the Soho Theatre, London, on 9 June 2011

Soho Theatre is supported by ACE, John Ellerman Foundation, Westminster City Council, Harold Hyam Wingate Foundation

Registered Charity No: 267234

CAST LIST

Stuart	Tim Treloar
Laura/Right-wing politician	Robyn Addison
Mother/Left-wing politician	Joanna Holden
Paul/Cat/Independent politician	Rocky Marshall
Father/Pundit	Barry McCarthy
Angie/Presenter	Golda Rosheuvel
Mullet	Shane Zaza

COMPANY

Director	Steve Marmion
Designer	Tom Scutt
Associate Designer	Oliver Townsend
Lighting Designer	Oliver Fenwick
Composer	Tom Mills
Casting Director	Nadine Rennie CDG
Set	Object Construction
Production Manager	Rich Blacksell
Costume Supervisor	Sydney Florence
Stage Manager	Martha Mamo
Deputy Stage Manager	Marie Costa
Assistant Stage Manager	Nicola Morris

BIOGRAPHIES

ROBYN ADDISON

Theatre includes:
THE RIVALS (Theatre Royal Bath/ West End); ABIGAIL'S PARTY (Zoo Venues); SINGIN' IN THE RAIN (Cambridge Arts Theatre); WILD HONEY, SUDDENLY LAST SUMMER, A MIDSUMMER NIGHT'S DREAM, A DELICATE BALANCE (ADC Theatre)

Television includes:
SURVIVORS (BBC); WATERLOO ROAD (BBC); GEORGE GENTLY (BBC); LIGHTNING STRIKES (WST Productions); CASUALTY (BBC); THE STREET (ITV Productions); DALZIEL AND PASCOE (BBC)

JOANNA HOLDEN

Theatre includes:
HANSEL & GRETEL (Kneehigh); THE 13 MIDNIGHT CHALLENGES OF ANGELUS DIABLO (RSC); QUEEN BEE (New Writing North); THE VENITIAN TWINS (Octagon Theatre); CIRQUE DU SOLEIL (International Tour); STUART LITTLE (Polka Theatre); MEETING MYSELF COMING BACK, THE MARK MAIER SHOW (Soho Theatre); THE CHILDREN'S HOUR, D'JUAN RETURNS (Royal National Theatre); THE KITCHEN (Royal Court); POND LIFE (Bush Theatre); PINOCCHIO, PLAY, EDMOND, THE OKLAHOMA OUTLAW, A BALLROOM OF ROMANCE, ROMEO & JULIET, A CLOCKWORK ORANGE, THE PRINCESS & THE GOBLIN, ANIMAL FARM (Northern Stage)

Television includes:
BYKER GROVE (BBC); FAKING IT (RDF/Channel 4)

Radio includes:
SIX GEESE ARE LAYING (Radio 4); ON THE BOX (Liberty Radio)

ROCKY MARSHALL

Theatre includes:
FAUSTUS (Headlong); RABBIT (Old Red Lion); PIAF (West End & Tour); MACBETH (Wimbledon Theatre); WHAT ABOUT LEONARDO (Lilian Baylis)

Television includes:
ZEN, WAKING THE DEAD, LAW & ORDER:UK, BONES, ROME, DALZIEL & PASCOE, HOLBY CITY, BAND OF BROTHERS, THE AFFAIR, EASTENDERS, CASUALTY, THE ROYAL, THE BILL, BUGS, LONDON'S BURNING

Film includes:
RE-KILL, MR WRIGHT, MEAN MACHINE, HART'S WAR and CLANCY'S KITCHEN.

BARRY MCCARTHY

Theatre includes:
THE WHITE GUARD (Royal National Theatre); REASON SEASON LIFE TIME (Almeida Theatre); ABSOLUTELY FRANK (Queen's Hornchurch); KEAN (Guildford/Tour/Apollo); THE CANTERBURY TALES (RSC/ Tour: Washington/Barcelona/ Almagro/Gielgud); CHILDREN OF A LESSER GOD (Salisbury); HAPPY BIRTHDAY, DEAR ALICE (Orange Tree/Stephen Joseph Theatre); AS YOU LIKE IT (RSC); THINGS WE DO FOR LOVE (Gielgud Theatre); THE SCARLET LETTER, THE GOVERNMENT INSPECTOR, KING LEAR, THE MASTER AND MARGARITA, A MIDSUMMER NIGHT'S DREAM, THE MERCHANT OF VENICE, THE COFFE HOUSE, SWAN SONG (Chichester); HOUSE AND GARDEN, BODY LANGUAGE, AND HENCEFORWARD... (Stephen Joseph Theatre)

Television includes:
THE BILL (Talkback Thames); DOCTORS (BBC); MISSING (BBC); HOLBY CITY (BBC); JUDGE JOHN DEED (BBC); PEAK PRACTICE (ITV); THE FINAL CUT (WGBH)

Film includes:
NOTES ON A SCANDAL (Fox Searchlight Films); KINKY BOOTS (Miramax Films); FOOD OF LOVE (Canal +); ERIK THE VIKING (Orion Pictures); BROTHERS AND SISTERS (BFI); LOVE AT FIRST SIGHT (Michael Davies Films); PRADA & PREJUDICE (Company)

GOLDA ROSHEUVEL

Trained: LONDON STUDIO CENTRE

Theatre includes:
THE TEMPEST, JULIUS CAESAR, ANTONY AND CLEOPATRA (Royal Shakespeare Company); MACBETH (Regents Park); JULIET AND HER ROMEO (Bristol Old Vic); ANGELS IN AMERICA, THE WINTER'S TALE (Headlong); THE BIBLE/THE FRONTLINE/ROMEO AND JULIET (The Globe); AMAZONIA (Young Vic); THE WHITE DEVIL (Menier Chocolate Factory); PURE GOLD (Soho Theatre); HAIR (The Gate); WE WILL ROCK YOU (Dominion Theatre); SOUTH PACIFIC (Royal National Theatre); JESUS CHRIST SUPERSTAR (Really Useful); TOMMY (Shaftesbury Theatre); CARMEN JONES (Old Vic Theatre); FAME (Victoria Palace/Aldwych Theatre); BABY ON BOARD (Stephen Joseph Theatre); SONGS FOR A NEW WORLD (The Bridewell).

Television includes:
LUTHER; HOLBY CITY; CONSUMING PASSION: 100 YEARS OF MILLS AND BOON; TRIAL AND RETRIBUTION; SILENT WITNESS; TORCHWOOD; CASUALTY; THE BILL

Radio includes:
THE UNDERSTANDING (BBC Radio 4); REGIME CHANGE (RSC/BBC3)

TIM TRELOAR

Theatre includes:
DUCHESS OF MALFI, VOLPONE (Greenwich Theatre); DOCTOR FAUSTUS, SCHOOL FOR SCANDAL (Greenwich Theatre); MACBETH (Chichester/West End/Broadway); TWELFTH NIGHT (Chichester); SING YER HEART OUT FOR THE LADS (Pilot Theatre Tour); THOMAS MORE, SEJANUS, BELIEVE WHAT YOU WILL, BACK TO METHUSELAH, RICHARD II, ROMEO AND JULIET, HAMLET, THE NIGHT BEFORE CHRISTMAS (Royal Shakespeare Company); HENRY V (Royal National Theatre); THE BEGGAR'S OPERA (Richmond Orange Tree) PENETRATOR (Latchmere); ROSE RAGE (Haymarket); MOUNTAIN LANGUAGE (Royal Court)

Television includes:
THE LIQUID BOMB PLOT (Raw Television); DOCTORS (BBC); FRAMED (BBC); SILENT WITNESS (BBC); LEWIS – THE POINT OF VANISHING (Granada); THE BILL (Talkback Thames); DOCTORS (BBC); CASUALTY (BBC); A TOUCH OF FROST (Granada); BOMBSHELL (Shed Productions); THE BRIEF (Carlton); MINE ALL MINE (Red Productions); SINGLE (Tiger Aspect); FOYLE'S WAR (Greenlit); MIDSOMER MURDERS (Bentley Productions); THE BENCH (BBC); BOMBER (Zenith Entertainment)

Film includes:
THE VIRGIN AND THE WARRIOR (Virgin and Warrior LLC); MACBETH (Illuminations); WONDROUS OBLIVION (Apt Films); LSD (Day and Night); MORNING HAS BROKEN (Dean Brothers)

SHANE ZAZA

Theatre includes:
PIECES OF VINCENT (Arcola Theatre); PETER PAN (NTS/Tour); MACBETH, ROMEO AND JULIET (The Globe); OXFORD STREET (Royal Court Theatre); MACBETH (West Yorkshire Playhouse); DEADEYE (Birmingham Rep/Soho Theatre); FURNACE FOUR (Soho Theatre); BILLY LIAR (Liverpool Playhouse); MERCURY FUR (Paines Plough); MINUTES PASS (Soho Theatre); GEORGE'S MARVELLOUS MEDICINE (Bolton Octagon); MASTER & MARGARITA, KES, THE ARBITRARY ADVENTURES OF AN ACCIDENTAL TERRORIST, NICHOLAS NICKLEBY (Lyric Hammersmith); THE LONG WAY HOME (New Perspectives); EAST IS EAST (New Vic Theatre)

Television includes:
COMING UP (Touchpaper TV); DOCTORS (BBC); MOUTH TO MOUTH (Avalon/BBC); THE OMID DJALILI SHOW (BBC); SPOOKS (BBC); TEN DAYS TO WAR (BBC); THE BILL (ITV); CASUALTY (BBC); WEIRDOS (Roughcut Television); MURPHY'S LAW (Tiger Aspect); WATCH OVER ME (Cattleprod Productions); DALZIEL & PASCOE (BBC); WATERLOO ROAD (BBC); MESSIAH (BBC)

Film includes:
CLEANSKIN (UK Film Studio); LOVE@1STSIGHT (1st Sight Films); THE DA VINCI CODE (Columbia Pictures)

ANTHONY NEILSON - WRITER

As A Writer/Director:
Theatre credits include: GET SANTA! (Royal Court); RELOCATED (Royal Court); REALISM (Edinburgh International Festival/Lyceum); THE WONDERFUL WORLD OR DISSOCIA (Tron/Edinburgh Lyceum/Theatre Royal Plymouth/ Royal Court/national tour); THE SEANCE (National Theatre Connections); THE MENU (National Theatre); THE LYING KIND (Royal Court); EDWARD GANT'S AMAZING FEATS OF LONELINESS (Theatre Royal, Plymouth and Headlong Theatre Company national tour); STITCHING - nominated Evening Standard Most Promising Newcomer (Traverse/ Bush); THE CENSOR – Writers' Guild Award for Best Fringe Play (Finborough/Royal Court); THE NIGHT BEFORE CHRISTMAS (Finborough); PENETRATOR (Edinburgh Festival/Finborough/ Royal Court); NORMAL: THE DUSSELDORF RIPPER (Edinburgh Festival/Finborough); THE YEAR OF THE FAMILY (Finborough); WELFARE MY LOVELY (Traverse)

As A Director:
Theatre credits include: THE BIG LIE (Latitude Festival), GOD IN RUINS (Soho Theatre), THE DRUNKS (Courtyard Theatre) all for the Royal Shakespeare Company; THE DEATH OF KLINGHOFFER – Herald Angel Award (Edinburgh International Festival/Scottish Opera). Forthcoming in Autumn 2011, a major revival of MARAT/ SADE for the Royal Shakespeare Company.

Film and television credits include: THE DEBT COLLECTOR – Winner of the Fipresci International Critics Award (Dragon Pictures/Film 4); SPILSBURY (Stone City/BBC), episodes of SPOOKS

STEVE MARMION - DIRECTOR

Steve is the Artistic Director of Soho Theatre.

Theatre includes:

Coming soon:
MONGREL ISLAND (Soho Theatre); ALADDIN (Lyric Hammersmith)

MACBETH (Open Air Theatre, Regents Park); EDWARD GANT'S AMAZING FEATS OF LONELINESS (Headlong/Soho Theatre); VINCENT RIVER (Brits off Broadway, New York); FAUSTUS (Headlong); METROPOLIS (Theatre Royal Bath); JACK AND THE BEANSTALK, DICK WHITTINGTON (Lyric Hammersmith); ONLY THE BRAVE, THE ENTIRE HISTORY OF CABARET, LATE NIGHT GIMP FIGHT (Edinburgh Festival); LOCK UP (National Theatre Education); TEMPEST 2000 (Sherman); A DATE TO REMEMBER (Soho Theatre); MAD MARGARET'S REVENGE (London One Act Festival/ Edinburgh Festival); MADAME BUTTERFLY'S CHILD (Pleasance/ Greenwich Festival/ Hong Kong Festival/ London One Act Festival - Winner of Best Overall Production/ Edinburgh Festival); CALIBAN'S ISLAND (Tour/ Edinburgh Festival); 97 - HILLSBOROUGH (Tour/ Edinburgh Festival); GHETTO (Watford Palace Theatre); LITTLE NELL, IMAGES OF A LONELY POETS WAR (E15); SLEEPING BEAUTY, MIRANDA'S MAGIC MIRROR, TINY TALES (Stephen Joseph Theatre, Scarborough); TEAM SPIRIT, SK8 – A HIP HOP MUSICAL, MULTIPLEX (Theatre Royal Plymouth)

TOM SCUTT - DESIGNER

Theatre includes:
THE MERCHANT OF VENICE, ROMEO AND JULIET (Royal Shakespeare Company); REMEMBRANCE DAY (Royal Court); SOUTH DOWNS/THE BROWNING VERSION (Chichester); HAMLET (Sheffield Crucible); THROUGH A GLASS DARKLY (Almeida); MOGADISHU (Royal Exchange, Manchester / Lyric Hammersmith); AFTER MISS JULIE (Salisbury Playhouse); PRESSURE DROP (On Theatre/ Wellcome Collection); DICK WHITTINGTON, JACK AND THE BEANSTALK (Lyric Hammersmith); THE CONTINGENCY PLAN – ON THE BEACH AND RESILIENCE (Bush Theatre); A MIDSUMMER NIGHT'S DREAM (Headlong); EDWARD GANT'S AMAZING FEATS OF LONELINESS (Headlong / Soho Theatre); VANYA, UNBROKEN and THE INTERNATIONALIST (Gate Theatre); BAY (Young Vic); THE MERCHANT OF VENICE (Octagon Theatre – Manchester Evening News 'Best Design' nomination); METROPOLIS (Theatre Royal Bath); HERE LIES MARY SPINDLER, THE THIRTEEN MIDNIGHT CHALLENGES OF ANGELUF DIABLO (RSC at Latitude Festival); THE COMEDY OF ERRORS (RWCMD/RSC); THE OBSERVER (design consultant, National Theatre Studio); PARADISE LOST (Southwark Playhouse); MAD FUNNY JUST (winner of the 2008 'Old Vic New Voices Award') and THE WATER HARVEST (Theatre 503); RETURN (Watford); BRANWEN (North Wales Stage); DOG TAGS (European Live Arts Network)

Opera includes: RIGOLETTO (Opera Holland Park)

Tom was awarded a 2007 Linbury Biennial Prize and the Jocelyn Herbert Award for Stage Design for his work with Headlong Theatre. He is an Associate Artist of Soho Theatre.

OLIVER TOWNSEND – ASSOCIATE DESIGNER

As Designer:
FINGS AIN'T WOT THEY USED T'BE (Union Theatre); 45 (Hampstead Theatre); THE BARBER OF SEVILLE (Opera Up Close); INTRIGUE/ LOVE (Southwark Playhouse); NARCISSUS (The Roundhouse); TWELTH NIGHT (The Faction Theatre); THE GRIMM BROS' CIRCUS (Bath Theatre Royal & En Masse Theatre); FOR ALL TIME, THE MEMORY OF WATER, BLACKBIRD, (Theatre By The Lake); L'ETOILE (Sherman Theatre)

In the role of Assistant, Associate, or Representative:
To Francis O'Connor: WRITTEN ON THE HEART, THE FLYING DUTCHMAN, MACBETH, IL TURCO IN ITALIA, SILENT NIGHT, VUT, BENZIN.
To Tom Scutt and Max Humphries: JACK AND THE BEANSTALK

OLIVER FENWICK – LIGHTING DESIGNER

Theatre includes:
THE HOLY ROSENBURGS, HAPPY NOW? (Cottesloe NT); RUINED (Almeida); DISCONNECT (Royal Court); A NUMBER (Menier Chocolate Factory); JULIUS CAESAR, THE DRUNKS, THE GRAIN STORE (RSC); KINGDOM OF EARTH, FABRICATION (The Print Room); GHOSTS, KEAN, THE SOLID GOLD CADILLAC, SECRET RAPTURE (all in the West End); THE CONTINGENCY PLAN, IF THERE IS I HAVEN'T FOUND IT YET (Bush Theatre); PRIVATE LIVES, THE GIANT, GLASS EELS, COMFORT ME WITH APPLES (Hampstead Theatre); RESTORATION (Headlong); LADY FROM THE SEA, SHE STOOPS TO CONQUER (Birmingham Rep); PURE GOLD (Soho Theatre); HAMLET, THE CARETAKER, COMEDY OF ERRORS, BIRD CALLS, IPHIGENIA (Crucible Theatre, Sheffield); THE CHAIRS (Gate Theatre); HENRY V, MIRANDOLINA (Royal Exchange); TIS PITY SHE'S A WHORE, THE DOLL'S HOUSE, HAY FEVER (West Yorkshire Playhouse); ENDGAME (Everyman Liverpool); SUNSHINE ON LEITH (Dundee Rep & Tour); NOISES OFF, ALL MY SONS, DR. FAUSTUS (Liverpool Playhouse); THE PICTURE (Salisbury Playhouse)

Opera credits include:
THE MERRY WIDOW (Opera North); SAMSEN ET DELILA, LOHENGRIN (Royal Opera House); THE TROJAN TRILOGY, THE NOSE (Linbury ROH); THE GENTLE GIANT (The Clore ROH).

TOM MILLS – COMPOSER

Theatre includes:
As Composer: MONGREL ISLAND (Soho Theatre); WANDERLUST (Royal Court); PERICLES, MACBETH (Open Air Theatre); DICK WHITTINGTON (also arranger, Lyric Hammersmith); PRINCE OF DENMARK (National Theatre Discover Programme); DITCH (Old Vic Tunnels); DUSK RINGS A BELL (HighTide Festival)

Other theatre as Composer and/or Sound Designer includes: HUIS CLOS (Donmar Warehouse season at Trafalgar Studios); MOONLIGHT AND MAGNOLIAS, GREAT EXPECTATIONS (Watermill); A MIDSUMMER NIGHT'S DREAM (Headlong Theatre); ELEKTRA (Young Vic/Gate Theatre); EDWARD GANT'S AMAZING FEATS OF LONELINESS (Headlong / Soho Theatre); THE ETERNAL NOT (Olivier Foyer, National Theatre);

OTHELLO (Assembly Rooms, Bath); ASSASSINS (Eyebrow Productions). He was music associate on Moscow Live, Lidless and Ditch for the 2010 HighTide Festival.

Credits as Composer and/or Musical Director includes BREATHING IRREGULAR, THE KREUTZER SONATA, UNBROKEN (Gate Theatre); OLIVER TWIST, THE JUNGLE BOOK, THE GRIMM BROTHER'S CIRCUS, METROPOLIS (The Egg, Theatre Royal Bath); RETURN TO THE FORBIDDEN PLANET (Bath Spa Music Society); BAND OF BLUES BROTHERS (Panthelion Productions)

THANK YOU

Hampstead Theatre, Donmar Warehouse and Lyric Hammersmith for props and costumes.

Katie Moore and Laura Metcalf for their work on costumes.

Lady Susie Sainsbury for all her support.

SOHO THEATRE

Soho Theatre is at the cutting edge of the bravest and most theatrical new writing.
We continue to produce new work, discover and nurture new writing, and target and develop new audiences.

Soho Theatre owns its own central London venue housing an intimate 150-seat theatre, a rehearsal and studio space, spaces for writers' development work and a lively bar and restaurant with a late licence.

We make, and offer the best work from across live performance in all its forms. Work, with brave new writers at its heart, that inspires, entertains, moves and challenges. Bold work, that takes risks and says difficult things in incredible ways.

Under the direction of new Artistic Director Steve Marmion Soho Theatre is pleased to announce a radical reworking of its building to create two new performance spaces that will sit above and below our permanent **Soho Theatre**.

Soho Theatre Upstairs
has become a dedicated space for emerging companies, new talent, young people and the most experimental new writing. A central London platform for anyone who has been tearing up the fringe.

Soho Theatre Downstairs
is a brand new, around table, dedicated comedy and cabaret venue in our basement - think 20s Berlin meets 50s new York meets 21st century Soho.

'The invaluable Soho Theatre'
MICHAEL BILLINGTON, GUARDIAN

'The capital's centre for daring international drama.'
EVENING STANDARD

'A jewel in the West End'
BBC LONDON

THE TERRACE BAR

Drinks can be taken into the auditorium and are available from the Terrace Bar on the second floor.

SOHO THEATRE ONLINE

Giving you the latest information and previews of upcoming shows, Soho Theatre can be found on facebook, twitter and youtube as well as at sohotheatre.com

EMAIL INFORMATION LIST

For regular programme updates and offers visit sohotheatre.com/mailing

HIRING THE THEATRE

An ideal venue for a variety of events, we have a range of spaces available for hire in the heart of the West End. Meetings, conferences, parties, civil ceremonies, rehearsed readings and showcases with support from our professional theatre team to assist in your events' success.

For more information, please see our website sohotheatre.com/hires or to hire space at Soho Theatre, email hires@sohotheatre.com and to book an event in Soho Theatre Bar, email sohotheatrebar@sohotheatre.com or ring 0207 434 9393.

Soho Theatre is supported by: ACE, John Ellerman Foundation, Westminster City Council, Harold Hyam Wingate Foundation

SOHO STAFF

Artistic Director: Steve Marmion
Executive Director: Mark Godfrey

BOARD OF DIRECTORS

Nicholas Allott (chair)
Sue Robertson (vice chair)
David Aukin
Oladipo Agboluaje
Norma Heyman
Shappi Khorsandi
Jeremy King
Lynne Kirwin
Neil Mendoza
David Pelham
Carolyn Ward
Roger Wingate

HONORARY PATRONS

Bob Hoskins - President
Peter Brook CBE
Simon Callow
Gurinder Chadha
Sir Richard Eyre CBE

ARTISTIC TEAM

Associate Director Nina Steiger

Soho Connect Director
Suzanne Gorman

Education Producer
Don McCamphill

Casting Director
Nadine Rennie CDG

Producer – Late Night Programme
Steve Lock
Theatre Producer Charlie Briggs

Senior Reader Sarah Dickenson

Writers' Centre Assistant
Julia Haworth

Associate Producer –
Comedy & Cabaret Lee Griffiths

ADMINISTRATION

General Manager Erin Gavaghan
Assistant to Directors Amanda Joy

Financial Controller Kevin Dunn
Finance Officer Kate Wickens

COMMUNICATIONS
Communications Director
Jacqui Gellman

Marketing Manager
Charlotte Simms

Press and Public Relations
Arthur Leone PR

Marketing & Digital Officer
Sarah Madden

Graphic Designer
Michael Windsor-Ungureanu

Marketing Interns Tilly Michell
& Rupert Dannreuther

DEVELOPMENT
Development Manager
Joanna Newell

Development Assistant
Hannah Bostock

BOX OFFICE AND FRONT OF HOUSE
Customer Services Manager
Julie Marshall

Acting Box Office Supervisor
Melinda Liu

Box Office Assistants Tristan Bernays, Amanda Collins, Paul Carroll, Dani Baker, Eniola Jaiyeoba, Hannah Cox, Hannah Gaunt, Jon Hampton, Helen Matthews, Leah Read, Louise Beere, Lynne Forbes, Melinda Liu, Tamsin Fessey, Will Sherriff-Hammond, Ellie Robinson & Molly White

Duty Managers Ian Irvine, Julia Haworth, Tara Kane and Martin Murphy

Front of House staff Emma Akwafo, Celyn Ebenezer, Janet Downer, Abby Forknall, Jonathan Hampton, Stephen Hoo, Marta Maroni, Jo Moore, Simon Perry, Indranyl Singharay, Joe Sirett, Hannah Steele, Molly White

PRODUCTION
Technical Manager Nick Blount
Senior Technician Natalie Smith
Technician Sam Smallman

**21 Dean Street,
London W1D 3NE
sohotheatre.com**

**Admin 020 7287 5060
Box Office 020 7478 0100**

THANK YOU

We are immensely grateful to our Sponsors, Principal Supporters, Soho Friends and Supporters for their commitment to Soho Theatre and our work.

Our supporters share with us a common goal and help us to achieve our mission: to source new work, to discover and nurture new talent and to produce profound and exciting theatre, comedy and cabaret.

Without your support, we would not be able to continue to achieve the diversity of our current programme, innovative community work and pioneering work through our Writer's Centre.

We gratefully acknowledge the following supporters who are an intrinsic part of Soho Theatre – thank you.

To find out how you can be involved in Soho Theatre, please contact the Development Team on 020 7478 0111 or email development@sohotheatre.com. Further information can also be found on our website www.sohotheatre.com.

Sponsors
Granta

Principal Supporter
Nicholas Allott
Daniel and Joanna Friel
Mr & Mrs Jack and Linda Keenan
Lady Susie Sainsbury
Mrs Carolyn Ward

Corporate Supporters
Cameron Mackintosh Ltd

In-Kind Sponsors
Latham & Watkins
The Groucho Club

Trusts
The Andor Charitable Trust
BBC Children in Need
City Bridge Charitable Trust
The David and Elaine Potter Foundation
The Earmark Trust
The John Ellerman Foundation
Equity Charitable Trust
Eranda Foundation
Esmée Fairbairn Foundation
St James's Piccadilly
Mackintosh Foundation
The Rose Foundation
The Foundation for Sport and the Arts
Sir Siegmund Warburg's Voluntary Settlement
The Harold Hyam Wingate Foundation
The Hazel Wood Charitable Trust
Westminster Arts

Soho Best Friends
David Day
Andrew & Jane McManus
Hannah Pierce
Nicola Stanhope

Soho Dear Friends
Natalie Bakova
Quentin Bargate
Anonymous

Soho Good Friends
Sarah & Neil Brener
David Brooks
Victoria Carr
Chris Carter
Jeremy Conway
Sharon Eva Degen
Geoffrey Eagland
Gail & Michael Flesch
James Hogan and Charles Glanville
Alban Gordon
Doug Hawkins
Laurence Humphreys-Davies
Etan Ilfeld
Jennifer Jacobs
Amanda Mason
Mr & Mrs Roger Myddelton
Linda O'Callaghan
Alan Pardoe
Gayle Rogers
Tom Schoon & Philippa Moore
Barry Serjent
Nigel Silby
Lesley Symons
Dr Sean White
Liz Young
Anonymous
Anonymous

Our other Friends:
Thank you also to the many Soho Friends we are unable to list here.

For a full list of our supporters, please visit sohotheatre.com

This list is correct as of Thursday 2 June 2011

Registered Charity: 267234

Realism

For Amy

Notes from the author

This edition has been revised to reflect the first major revival of Realism *in the UK, at the Soho Theatre in London, 2011. Scene Three – which previously focused on the introduction of the smoking ban – has been rewritten in a way that keeps it relevant, yet preserves the essence of the staging. Inevitably, however, this section will begin to date the play, which may cause problems for future productions. Anyone attempting a production and finding this section problematic should get in touch with me via the publishers.*

Those watching the revival will notice that the names of the characters Stuart and Paul will be changed to the names of the actors playing those parts. Similarly, the real actor's name should be used when mentioned in the aforementioned Scene Three, as one of the panellists. The rationale for this is that these are characters who actually appear in the 'real time' of the play. On this basis, you might argue that Angie and our poor 'cold-caller' should be treated similarly. And you might – I emphasise 'might' – be right. I leave it up to you.

Finally, I should just re-emphasise that this play is only a blueprint for potential productions. These parts were written for specific actors and utilised in-jokes and colloquialisms that may not translate to every locale. Identify the important elements of a scene and preserve them, but otherwise you should feel at liberty to change the dialogue as you need. In particular, you should find ways to naturalise the opening exchange between your various Stuarts and Pauls. They are long-time friends and have an ease between them. Allow your actors to improvise their way to an approximation of the scene.

What follows is the original preface to the text . . .

While the dialogue in this play is largely my own, the material herein was hugely influenced by the suggestions, criticisms and improvisations of the actors and creative team, whose names are listed in the text.

As ever, what follows is a record of a show that was presented in 2006. Elements of the sound or production design may be described, but should only be taken into account; they represent no stipulation on my part (except where indicated).

The play contains references to topical events, localised matters and personal issues that may limit its relevance in other territories or times. Where possible, I have attempted to explain the dramatic relevance of these moments so that the imaginative translator may find a way to adapt them.

Though *Realism* is divided into acts, it should be presented without an interval.

Please note that though there are several phone conversations during the play, at no point should a phone ever be present (or represented) onstage.

THE SET

In the original production, the stage was raked from front to back with a slight imbalance upstage left.

All the elements of a normal home were present. From front of stage to back: a sofa, a fridge with work surface, a washing machine, a toilet, a bed, a dining table and chairs, an armchair, etc. Various practical lights (both standing and hanging) were also arranged around the set.

However, the stage itself was covered with several tons of off-white sand. All of the aforementioned furniture was cut off to varying degrees (and at varying angles) so as to appear 'sunk' into this sand. The television was placed at the very front of the stage, seeming almost completely submerged, allowing only enough space to use it as a lighting source for the sofa.

The walls on all three sides consisted of large pillars, grey and textured, which hinted at concrete. Actors entered and exited between them.

PRE-SHOW

As the audience arrived, we played a medley of UK traditional tunes which was famously (until 2006) used as the opening music for BBC Radio 4. It not only set the play's beginning firmly in the morning; it also inspired a spirit of joviality, which I would recommend – as *Realism* is, to all intents and purposes, a comedy. If you have any kind of equivalent – a light tune that your audience finds synonymous with morning – I would respectfully suggest that you consider its use.

'Breakdowns' are presented in square brackets at the scene beginnings. These describe what is actually occurring in the play's 'real' time-line. I wrote them for my own benefit and present them for your interest only. You may prefer not to read them, and experience the show in the same vague sense of confusion that the audience did.

Characters

Stuart
Paul
Mother
Father
Mullet
Angie
Presenter
Pundit
Right-Wing Politician
Left-Wing Politician
Independent Politician
Audience Member
Laura
Minstrel 1
Minstrel 2
Minstrel 3
Simon
Cat
Bystanders

Act One: Morning

One

[*In which . . .* **Stuart** *gets a phone call from his friend* **Paul**. **Paul** *wants him to come and play football.* **Stuart** *declines the offer. He puts out some food for the cat. He remembers a dream he had the previous night. He goes back to bed.*]

Stuart *sits on the couch, in his bedclothes. He has one hand down his pants, absent-mindedly squeezing himself – it is not a sexual gesture. He looks very tired.*

Paul, *wearing a suit, is looking in the fridge.* (*Note: at no point in the following scene do the actors make eye contact.*)

Paul Did I wake you?

Stuart No, not really.

Paul Not really?

Stuart I was awake.

Paul Were you still in bed?

Stuart *smells his fingers.*

Stuart Yeah, well, it's Saturday morning so . . .

Paul So I woke you up. I'm sorry.

Pause.

Stuart What's going on?

Paul Were you out last night?

Stuart For a while.

He tries to look at a birthmark on his shoulder. It's itching.

Paul D'you get pissed?

Stuart A bit.

Paul A bit?

Stuart Paul – I've not even had a cup of tea –

Paul I was just wondering what you're up to. You playing fives later?

He starts dribbling a football back and forward.

Stuart I don't know. I don't think so.

Paul You've got to.

Stuart Why have I got to?

Paul We're already a man down.

Stuart I don't think I can.

Paul Why not?

Stuart I just – I don't really feel like it.

Pause.

Paul What do you feel like, then?

Stuart What?

Paul What do you feel like doing?

Stuart Not much.

Paul Aw, come on – come and play footie. We'll have a few pints.

For the first time we see **Paul** *from the front. His shirt is half open and his suit jacket has vomit down it.*

Stuart I really don't feel like it.

Paul So what are you going to do? Just mope about your flat all day?

Stuart I've got stuff to do.

Paul Like what?

Stuart Just boring things.

Paul Like what?

Stuart For fuck's sake . . .

Paul I'm just asking.

Stuart Like washing, cleaning up – domestic shit.

Paul You can do that tomorrow.

Stuart I can't.

Paul Why not?

Stuart Cos I just – I haven't got any clean clothes . . . I just need to get myself together.

Paul *crosses to the couch and sits beside* **Stuart**.

Paul I could come over after. Get a few cans in. Get a DVD out.

He instantly falls asleep. During the next exchange, he nods in and out of consciousness.

Stuart Paul, I really – I just want to do nothing.

Paul You want to do nothing?

Stuart Yeah, I just –

Paul We don't have to do anything. We can just kiss and cuddle a bit; there's no pressure.

Stuart That's tempting.

Pause.

No, really, I just – I said to myself I was just going to do nothing today. It's been a fucking hellish week at work and I'm just knackered; just want to chill out.

Paul What good – do you?

Stuart Eh?

Paul That going to – ?

Pause. Annoyed, **Stuart** *stands. Damned reception.*

Stuart Fucking things.

Paul I said what good's it going to do you, moping about your flat all day?

Stuart I'm not going to be moping.

Paul You are – you're going to mope.

Stuart I'm not going to mope.

Paul Mope, mope, mope; that'll be you.

Stuart Right, well, so if I want to mope I can fucking mope, can't I? I mean, I'm not planning on moping but I reserve the right to mope in my own fucking house.

Paul All right, all right; calm down, calm down. I just don't want you getting all depressed.

Stuart I'm not, I'm fine.

Paul All right.

Stuart Just want to spend a bit of time on my own.

Paul Fair enough.

He staggers to his feet.

Will I give you – tomorrow?

Stuart Will you give me tomorrow?

Paul (*louder*) Will I give you a *shout* tomorrow?

Stuart Yeah, give me a shout tomorrow.

Paul If you change your mind –

Stuart I'll give you a bell.

Paul Give us a bell. We'll be in the Duck's Arse from about five.

Stuart All right, cheers.

Paul *exits.*

Pause. **Stuart** *yawns.*

Stuart *goes to the fridge, opens it. He takes out a tin of cat food and prises back the lid. He fills a bowl with food. Some of it drops onto the floor. At the top of his voice he shouts:*

Here, kitty kitty kitty kitty!

He considers staying awake, but then walks back towards his bedroom.

On the way, his **Mother** *appears. He stops.*

Mother Have you seen the sky?

Stuart What do you mean?

Mother It's full of bombers.

Stuart Where from?

Mother Israel? [*At the time of writing, in 2006, Israel had invaded Lebanon. Substitute a more topical/timeless reference if necessary.*]

Pause. **Stuart** *continues on his way.*

Mother *takes a seat at the dining table.*

Stuart *climbs back into bed.*

Lights fade. Music – during which **Father** *enters, carrying a morning paper. He takes a seat at the dining table, handing part of the paper to* **Mother**. *They read.*

Two

[**Stuart** *gets up again. He remembers another fragment of a dream. He makes himself a cup of tea, and gets a mild electric shock from the toaster. Feeling bad about himself, he attempts to exercise but ends up pretending to be a rabbit. He remembers a friend chasing him with a shit-covered stick. The same friend got him to taste a crayon, which was horrible. He watches a news report about the Middle East crisis.*]

Stuart *wakes up with cramp. He hits the side of his leg. The pain passes. Pause.*

Paul *enters behind* **Stuart**, *carrying a huge carrot.* **Stuart** *doesn't see him.*

Paul Stuart.

Stuart What?

Paul That fucking squirrel's back.

Stuart What does he want?

Paul He wants his guts back in.

Stuart That'll cost a fortune.

Paul Yeah, but Angie'll pay for it. She's on her way out.

Paul *sits in the armchair.*

Stuart *gets up and collects a cup from the cupboard.*

Father Stuart, don't bother me.

On his way to the fridge, **Stuart** *looks inside the cup, checking that it's clean. He turns on the electric kettle.*

Mother Can you see it? There – a castle, look. The tea leaves make a turret, and the tea's like a moat at the bottom.

Stuart What's a moat?

Mother It's the water round a castle, to keep the folk from getting in.

Simultaneously, **Mother** *and* **Stuart** *sing a fairly buoyant, very British wartime song – the sort of song a mother used to sing:*

> I like a nice cup of tea in the morning,
> I like a nice cup of tea with my tea . . .

But **Mother**'*s voice fades away, leaving* **Stuart** *groping for the lyrics. A sound arrives, punching into him the realisation of her absence.*

Stuart *takes a moment to recover, then puts the cup down. He looks at the jars in front of him.*

Stuart Coffee – tea? Tea – coffee?

Stuart *opens a box of tea bags. He drops a tea bag into the cup.*

He opens the fridge.

He takes out a packet of bread. He snaps off two pieces and pushes them into the toaster. He takes some milk out of the fridge. He smells the milk.

The sound of children playing

The sound of the water boiling in the kettle becomes the sound of horses galloping. It reaches a crescendo . . . then stops.

He pours the hot water into the mug.

Smoke is beginning to rise from the toaster. The bread is trapped in there.

Stuart *tries to get the toaster to eject the toast but it isn't working. He's beginning to panic.*

Mullet *appears behind the couch. He looks like a child from the seventies. He is hyperactive and extremely irritating.*

Mullet (*in an annoying sing-song voice*) Stewpot! Stewpot! Stewpot! [*This is what many children called Stuart were nicknamed in the seventies.*]

Stuart For fuck's sake, what?!

Mullet The toast's burning!

Stuart I know! I can't get it out.

Mullet Use a knife!

Stuart I'll get electrocuted.

Mullet You won't.

Panicked, **Stuart** *runs to the cutlery drawer and runs back to the toaster.*

He plunges the knife into the toaster and is immediately thrown on to his back by the resulting shock. **Mullet** *finds this hilarious.*

Mullet (*gleeful*) You fucking knob!

Angrily, **Stuart** *smacks the toaster off the surface.*

Mullet That was a fucking beauty!

Stuart My heart's going like the clappers!

Pause.

Fucking hell.

He picks up the toaster and the burnt toast. He takes a knife to the toast and starts to scrape off the burnt bits.

Angie *appears behind him, wearing a dressing gown. She stops, annoyed.*

Angie Why do you do that?

Stuart What?

Angie Scrape the fucking toast into the sink?

Stuart I don't like burnt toast.

Angie So scrape it into the fucking bin! It just clogs the sink up. And then you smear it on the side of the Flora [*a type of margarine*]. You're a dirty bastard.

She continues across the stage.

Stuart I thought you were going to call me?

She exits.

Pause. **Stuart** *throws the toast into the pedal bin.*

He walks over to the sofa, sits down.

Stuart I've broke out in a sweat from that shock.

Mullet That was a beauty. You went fucking flying!

Stuart *tries to look at his mole.*

Mullet What's wrong?

Stuart That birthmark's itching.

Mullet Let's see.

He takes a look at it.

I'm not joking, man; that's cancer.

Stuart It's not cancer. I'm too young to have cancer.

Mullet You're joking, aren't you? Fucking Kylie's got cancer – look how young she is! If someone with all that money and an arse like that can get cancer, you think you can't? What else is wrong with you?

Stuart My left eye's still funny.

Mullet That's diabetes.

Stuart It's not diabetes!

He goes to the mirror, distressed. Behind him, **Mullet** *makes faces and rude signs.*

Mullet Why not? Your uncle had it.

Stuart Doesn't mean I've got it.

Mullet So why are you thirsty all the time?

Stuart Am I thirsty all the time?

He thinks about it.

I'm thirsty a lot of the time. And I keep getting cramp. Is that diabetes?

Mullet (*mimics*) 'Is that diabetes?' You're such a fucking jessie.

Stuart Fuck you.

Mullet What's happened to you, man? You were going to be a choo-choo driver. You were going to be an astronaut. What's happened to that guy? What's happened to the guy who was going to build a rocket and fly to fucking Mars? I mean, look at yourself. What do you see?

Pause.

Stuart A fat fucking shite.

Mullet A fat fucking shite. And how do you feel?

Stuart Like shite.

Mullet Like shite. And what are you going to do about it?

Stuart Fuck all.

Mullet You're going to do fuck all. You could have gone out to play footie but you're going to sit around the house all day moping and why? Because of a girl! Because you're waiting for a girl to call you!

Stuart I can't help it. I love her.

Mullet (*mimics*) 'I loooove her'! So why did you dump her then?

Stuart I didn't.

Mullet You did. You dumped her because she had horrible, wobbly thighs and a wonky fucking nose.

Stuart Shut your stupid face.

Mullet It's true.

Stuart It's not!

Pause.

Mullet Hey, Stu – do that thing with your pants!

Pause. **Stuart** *pulls his pants up over his belly. Cranking one arm, he lets his belly extend to its full size, as if pumping it up. Then he removes an imaginary cork from his belly and lets it deflate.*

Mullet *That* – is fucking *genius*.

Stuart I'm a fat sack of shit.

Mullet So what? So's Tony Soprano and he gets shags. And you know why? Because only poofs care what they look like. And women know that.

Stuart *gets on to the floor.*

Mullet What are you doing? Are you going to do press-ups? Only wanks do press-ups.

Stuart *starts doing press-ups.*

Stuart I'm not listening to you.

Mullet *gets down beside him and moves and talks in rhythm with* **Stuart***'s increasingly laboured exercises.*

Mullet Good. So you won't hear me say how *boring* they are, and what a *poof* you are, and how *boring* they are, and what a *wank* you are, and how boring they are, and how *fat* you are, and what a *weakling* you are –

Stuart *gives up, knackered and exasperated, and strangely amused.*

Mullet How many was that?

Stuart Four. (*Or however many he managed.*)

Mullet *derides him.*

Mullet Four! You only managed four?!

Stuart I'm going to build them up over time.

He stands up and starts to jump up and down, on the spot.

Mullet Look at you now! You look like a fucking rabbit!

Stuart Do I?

Mullet (*excited*) Do this – Stu – do this.

Hopping alongside **Stuart**, **Mullet** *makes paws with his hands and sticks his teeth out.*

Mullet Like a rabbit!

Stuart *does it.*

Mullet Are you hungry, rabbit?

Stuart *nods.*

Mullet You want some carrots?

Stuart *nods.*

Mullet Say, 'I want some carrots, Mr Farmer.'

Stuart 'I want some carrots, Mr Farmer.'

Mullet *offers his crayons.*

Mullet Right – Imagine these are carrots! Come and get the carrots.

Stuart *follows after* **Mullet**.

Mullet No, but you have to hop.

Stuart *hops after him.*

Mullet That's it – come and get the carrots, Thumper!

Stuart *reaches him but* **Mullet** *suddenly produces a stick.*

Stuart What's that?

Mullet It's a stick!

Stuart What's on the end of it?

Mullet Keich! [*Scottish slang for shit.*]

Stuart Fuck off – is it?

Mullet Smell it.

Tentatively **Stuart** *does – he gags.*

Stuart Aw, fuck off!

Grinning, **Mullet** *chases after him.*

Stuart Fuck off! Fuck off, ya dirty bastard!

They run around laughing, and occasionally gagging.

Mullet *whoops like a Red Indian and suddenly lots of others appear, as if in a playground. He chases them all around and for a moment the stage is full of noise and activity. One by one they claim sanctuary by the walls. Finally, out of breath,* **Stuart** *is cornered.*

Stuart Put that down.

Mullet Why?

Stuart (*gags*) Just put it down. I'm telling you.

Mullet Telling me what?

Stuart Telling you to put it down.

Mullet *thrusts the shitty stick at him.*

Stuart You better fucking not – I'm telling you.

Mullet You want the carrots? Are you going to hop to the carrots?

Stuart I'll hop to the carrots if you put it down.

Pause. **Mullet** *puts the stick down.*

Stuart *advances a little.* **Mullet** *quickly picks the stick up and thrusts it at him again.*

Stuart Put the fucking thing down!

Mullet All right, all right – I'm putting it down.

He puts it down, then throws the orange crayons.

Hop to the carrots, rabbit.

Stuart *hops over to the carrots.*

Mullet Eat one.

Pause. **Stuart** *eats the end of one. He spits it out in disgust.*

Stuart That's fucking awful!

The game's over – **Stuart** *sits on the couch.*

Mullet Stewpot! Stuart! Stuart.

Stuart *ignores him.*

He picks up his tea and sips it. He turns the TV on – its light plays on his face.

Dejected, **Mullet** *gathers up his things and leaves, dragging his stick behind him.*

The sounds of war.

Behind him, people run screaming as if under heavy fire, taking shelter behind the appliances.

Oblivious to them, **Stuart** *crosses to the fridge and fixes himself a bowl of cereal.*

He arrives back at the couch as the same time as the others, who assemble themselves around him.

Three

[**Stuart** *gets annoyed by a radio discussion show. A pirate radio station interferes with the reception. He imagines himself as part of the panel. He considers how to get* **Angie** *to call.*]

Right-Wing Politician Well, look – they used to say fat was a feminist issue but these days I'm afraid it's a financial one, as much as anything. The fact is, obesity costs the NHS nearly six billion pounds a year. Six billion pounds. And that's at current levels. By the year 2040, the estimate is that nearly half the adults in Britain will be obese.

Left-Wing Politician And half the children.

Right-Wing Politician Well – a quarter of children is the projection, but still – that's a simply unsustainable burden. So it seems to me that anything we can do to stem that particular / um – tide –

Left-Wing Politician Paying doctors to tell people they're fat?

Applause from the audience. **Stuart** *sits on the couch, eating a bowl of cereal. The panellists are arranged around him, on the same couch.*

Right-Wing Politician Well – that's a simplistic way of um – expressing that policy –

Left-Wing Politician No it isn't, that's exactly what you're proposing –

Presenter Let (*insert name of actor*) finish what she's saying. We'll come to you.

Right-Wing Politician It's part of a whole raft of policies that we want to introduce, including regulation for the food industry –

Left-Wing Politician Yes but nobody's in favour of obesity. But what the Tories always miss – and now their liberal cheerleaders it would seem –

The sound of a pirate radio station cuts in – booming dance music.

Stuart Oh fuck . . .

In unison, **Stuart** *and the panel members crab-walk across the stage, stopping here and there, until the reception returns.*

Left-Wing Politician . . . is that obesity is fundamentally linked to issues like unemployment and poverty.

And then, gingerly, so as not to lose reception, they all back on to the couch, as one, and resume their positions.

Pundit Oh poppycock –

Left-Wing Politician You try –

Pundit It's poppycock!

Left-Wing Politician You try feeding a family of five for a week on / jobseekers' allowance –

Pundit Well, you shouldn't have a family of five, should you? If you can't afford it, don't have a family of five. I mean, I grew up in a large family and we ate – we didn't eat like kings but we ate healthily. We ate home-grown vegetables –

Stuart Oh, you arsehole –

Left-Wing Politician Oh, come on –

Pundit People are fat because they eat too much. It's as simple as that. They eat too much and they sit on their behinds all day and I don't see why the NHS, such as it is, should have to pay for – stomach staples and whatever else simply because they can't control themselves –

Stuart Oh fuck off.

Pundit I beg your pardon?!

Stuart I said fuck off, you greasy fascist twat.

Left-Wing Politician Hear, hear.

Stuart And you can shut up and all. What's your idea? Banning cakes?

Left-Wing Politician No –

Stuart Well you banned smoking.

Left-Wing Politician Yes, well –

Stuart I mean, Jesus Christ – a Labour Government and you banned smoking. I'm a middle-aged guy. I work like a bastard all year round. I don't have kids, wouldn't fucking see them hardly if I did – I'm not married, I pay a shitload of tax every year and I get fuck all in return. I had one tiny pleasure in life – a pint in the pub and a cigarette. And you wouldn't even let me have that. And now you want to hassle me about being fat? Do you know why I'm fucking fat? Do you?

Murmurs of 'No'.

Because I gave up fucking smoking!!

Some applause. He gets up and goes to the fridge for more milk for his cereal.

I didn't give up because I wanted to. I gave up because I might as well have had a yellow-fucking-star pinned to my chest.

Presenter And because your sperm was watery.

Stuart Yes, that's right! I thought my sperm was too watery. I thought maybe smoking was responsible. And guess what? It wasn't! It was all a lie! I don't feel more energetic, I can't taste anything better, I still get out of breath and – despite the supposedly increased blood circulation – my once proud, ten p.m. erection still hangs forlornly at twenty-five to nine.

The smoking ban wasn't about health, you see. If it was about health, they would have banned smoking outright. Imagine if they found out fucking . . . Pot Noodle was so toxic that just being *in the same building* as someone eating it was potentially fatal? Would they have kept it on the shelves?

Applause. Warming to his theme, he takes the aspect of a lawyer.

No – the smoking ban, ladies and gentlemen, was about humiliation. Smokers were just the next in a long line –

He stands in the cat food. Disgusted, he scrapes it from his foot, while continuing.

In a long line of . . . state-approved scapegoats fed to this fractured, dysfunctional, post-Thatcherite society to lend it some semblance of cohesion. Cohesion through intolerance. Superiority through condemnation. When empathy is dead, only hatred will bind.

Huge applause, as if it was a speech by Lincoln. And now there's a slight echo on his voice, as if he's addressing thousands:

In summing up – I can put it no better than the famous poem written by some Jewish guy. Or possibly a German.

> When they came for the gays, I did not speak out. Because I was not a – gayboy. Though I'm not at all against it. I'm just not one.
>
> When they came for the fox hunters, I did not speak out. Because I was not a toffee-nosed twat on a horse with a little trumpet.
>
> When they came for the smokers, I did not speak out. Because I was not a yellow-fingered ashtray weasel.
>
> But then they came for me.
>
> And there was no one left to speak out.

And with this, **Stuart** *passes his empty cereal bowl to the* **Right-Wing Politician** *and makes his way to the bed.*

A stunned pause and then, one by one, the panellists begin to clap, and the audience begins to clap, and then the panellists stand, and so does the audience. The response is tumultuous.

Right-Wing Politician Who was that man?

Pundit I don't know, but he's turned my head around, I'll tell you that!

Independent Politician He's turned everyone's head around!

The **Presenter** *attempts to get the audience to calm down.*

Presenter All right, thank you, ladies and gentlemen, can we – ?

But now there is a thumping of chairs.

No please – please put down the furniture –

At this point, someone from the audience rushes up to the stage and throws a chair at the **Presenter**.

Audience Member Fascist bastards!

The chair just misses her. The **Audience Member** *runs out of the doors.*

Presenter Ladies and gentlemen, please stay calm! Please, no smoking, please – please don't light those – don't light that cigarette!

Smoke begins to curl onto the stage. The panellists begin to cough and splutter.

(*To panellists.*) I think we should go. (*To the audience.*) Ladies and gentlemen – listeners at home – I'm afraid we have no choice but to abandon this week's *Any Questions* due to a stunningly lucid intervention from a member of the public!

Left-Wing Politician (*into mobile*) Get me the Prime Minister. (*Pause.*) I don't care about that – get him on the phone right now!

Pundit Keep to the floor where there's air!

They drop to the floor and start to crawl away, a riot occurring in the audience.

Presenter Next week we'll be in Stevenage – so if you want tickets for that visit our website or call us on 0800-777-444 –

A fireman enters (*the actor playing* **Mullet**), *his torchlight casting a beam through the smoke.*

Mullet We've got to go now!

He lifts the **Presenter** *over his shoulder and carries her out.*

Presenter And don't forget *Any Answers* after the break –

She is taken away.

Through the smoke, **Stuart** *is illuminated, sitting cross-legged on the end of his bed. His pot belly makes him look like Buddha.*

The sounds of the audience riot fade.

As the smoke clears, he stands and walks to the front of the stage.

He peers out at the audience, as if looking in a mirror.

Stuart *says only a few of the following statements out loud. The rest are played on tape, creating a collage of sound. During this,* **Angie** *crosses the stage at the back in her dressing gown, towelling her hair; and the* **Right-Wing Politician** *takes her clothes off – she is wearing a nightdress underneath, and now becomes* **Laura**.

Stuart It's me.
It's Stuart.
It's me again.
I know you're ignoring me.
I know you don't want to speak to me.
I need to speak to you.
I've got some things of yours.
You've got some things of mine.
You should come and get them.
I should come and collect them.
Please call me.
Will you call me?
As soon as you get this.
When you've got the time.
Today if possible.
I'll be in.
Or try my mobile.
But we need to talk.
I'd like to talk.
It'd be good to talk.
I miss you.

I love you.
I made a mistake.
It won't take long.
It's really urgent.
Please.
Please call me.

The smoke clears to reveal **Laura**, *sitting on the toilet.*

Four

[**Stuart** *lies in bed thinking. He tries to masturbate. He hears an ice-cream van outside and contemplates buying one; instead he opens some mail. It is a bill for the council tax. He makes up a little song. He takes a shit. He takes a shower.*]

Stuart What are you doing?

Laura What does it look like I'm doing?

Stuart Number twos?

Laura No.

Stuart Number threes?

Laura What's number threes?

Stuart Both.

Laura No, just number ones.

Pause.

Get out then.

Stuart Why?

Laura What do you mean, why? Cos I can't pee with you . . . standing there.

Stuart Why not?

Laura Cos I just can't. I can't pee with anyone in the room.

Stuart Try.

Laura No!

Stuart (*mimics*) 'No!'

Laura Stuart . . .

Stuart Do you not love me?

Laura Yes. What's that got to do with it?

Stuart 'What's love got to do, got to do with it?'

Laura 'What's love but a second-hand emotion?'

Stuart Do you not trust me?

Laura Yes. Sort of.

Stuart Sort of?

Laura Look, it doesn't matter if I trust you or not, I still can't do the toilet with you sitting there! I can't even do it with my sister in the room.

Stuart There's lots of stuff you do with me that you wouldn't do with your sister. Well – outside of my masturbatory fantasies.

Laura You're disgusting. Do you really think about that?

Stuart What?

Laura About me doing things with my sister?

Stuart *shrugs.*

Laura What sort of things?

Stuart Just being tender and sisterly with each other. Sometimes using a double-ended dildo.

Laura That's disgusting. You're a dirty old perv.

Pause. He's not leaving.

Please – I'm really desperate.

Stuart Can't be that desperate.

Pause.

Two people that love each other – they should be able to pee in the same room.

Laura See that's where we differ. I don't think peeing has anything to do with love.

Stuart I don't want you to piss on my face. I just want you to pee with me here in the room.

Laura But why, though?

Stuart I don't know. Because it's something you've never done with anyone else.

Pause.

Laura I don't think I can.

Stuart Try.

Pause. He makes a peeing sound.

Laura I don't think I can.

Stuart Are you worried you'll fart?

Laura No!

Stuart It's all right. Sometimes you need to kick-start the bike. I understand.

Laura I'm not worried I'm going to fart!

Pause.

Stuart Just think of cool, clear water. Flowing. A rushing brook. Niagara Falls. Waves crashing against the pier.

She tries. Pause. A trickle.

Oh – something's happening . . .

Pause. He puts his hand between her legs.

Laura No, it'll stop.

Stuart I just want to feel it.

Pause.

I love everything that comes out of you.

He starts to touch her. She hugs him.

Enter **Angie**.

Angie What's going on here then?

Music. Bad porn music.

They stop, startled. **Laura** *is still aroused.*

Angie You don't have a fucking clue what you're doing. Get out of the way.

She pushes **Stuart** *aside and thrusts her hand between* **Laura***'s legs.*

Angie I'll show you how the little bitch likes it.

Laura *starts to breathe heavily. She clings on to* **Angie**.

Angie That's it, you little slut. You like that?

Someone in the bed starts to masturbate.

This is how to do it.

Laura Oh yes, oh yes, that's it – oh finger me, finger me.

Angie (*to* **Stuart**) Do something useful with yourself and spank my fucking arse.

Stuart *starts to spank* **Angie***'s arse.*

Angie That's it – spank my big fucking arse!

Mother *appears.*

Mother Does this dress look terrible on me?

Laura Oh God, that's so good – oh finger me!

Mother I've got a bum like a baby elephant.

Stuart (*to* **Mother**) Go away!

Angie Spank my big fucking arse!

Mother It wobbles like a big bloody jelly.

Stuart (*and the bed-wanker simultaneously*) Go away!

Laura Oh that's it, that's it, just there –

Angie Spank me harder, you fucking bastard!

Mother What do you want for your Christmas?

Laura Oh God, that's good – rub my little cunt!

Mother I've got a bum like a baby elephant's.

Mother *slaps her bottom. The rhythm falls into time with* **Stuart**'*s spanking of* **Angie**.

Angie Spank my big elephant bum!

Laura What do you want for your Christmas?

Mother What do you want for your Christmas?

Angie What do you want for your Christmas, then?

Furious, **Stuart** *gives up. Simultaneously, the girls go limp like dolls and* **Stuart**'*s 'double' swings up, out of the bed, to sit on its edge.*

Stuart (*to* **Mother**) Will you stop going on about your arse?! I don't want to think about your arse! It makes me want to vomit! I don't go on to you about my fucking balls, do I?! How would you like that?!

Pause. He sits on the end of the bed, mirrored in posture by his double.

Pause.

I'm sorry.

Mother It's all right.

Pause.

Stuart You know that aftershave stuff you bought me?

Mother The stuff you said was cheap shite?

Stuart I know, I know, but listen: I've still got it. And you know, if there was a fire, I wouldn't save my CDs first or my iPod or anything; the first thing I'd save would be that aftershave.

Mother Don't be silly. If there's a fire you just get on with saving yourself.

Stuart Well, obviously, yes, but – I'm trying to tell you something. I'm trying to tell you what it means to me.

Pause.

It's funny that, isn't it? Of all the really nice things you gave me – it's the cheap shite that means the most.

Pause.

Will *you* tell her to call me?

Pause. The sound of an ice-cream van. **Laura** *leaves.* **Angie** *bends over the toilet and vomits.* **Stuart** *kneels beside her, rubbing her back.* **Mullet** *bursts in.*

Mullet Ice cream, ice cream, we all scream for ice scream!

Stuart Too old for ice cream.

Mullet What then?

Stuart Don't know. Sorbet?

Mullet Fucking sorbet! You're such an old wank! I'll bet you're even starting to like ready-salted!

Stuart I am, actually.

Mullet Come on – let's get some ice cream! A 99. Or a push-up.

Stuart They probably don't have any ice cream. It's probably just smack.

Mullet Get some of that then.

Stuart I'll become an addict.

Mullet So?

Stuart So then we'll have to live in rubble. You wouldn't like that, would you?

Mullet You're so boring and fat and emotionally stunted! Go and see if the post's here.

Stuart *looks at his watch.*

Stuart Fucking should be.

Mullet Go on then!

Stuart It'll just be bills.

Mullet It might not be. It might be a birthday card.

Stuart It's not my birthday.

Mullet So?

Pause. They exit, in a kind of synchronicity.

A light breeze blows sand across the stage. The light bulbs sway.

Stuart *enters, opening a bill.*

He stops, and reads it.

Stuart What the fuck . . . ?

Pause.

I fucking paid that!

He throws it in the bin and puts the kettle on again. Pause.

What a bunch of cunts.

As he waits for the kettle to boil, he repeats the phrase, singing it to himself.

What a bunch of cunts, what a bunch of cunts . . .
What a bunch of cunts, what a bunch of cunts . . .

Music begins. He sings along, the orchestration becoming more elaborate.

Behind him, female dancers appear.

He becomes involved in a song-and-dance number. The lyrics consist only of the words 'What a bunch of cunts' and sometimes 'What a bunch of fucking cunts' for variety's sake.

Male dancers join in – they are blacked-up, like Al Jolson.

[*Note: those of us who grew up in Britain in the seventies were treated, on Saturday nights, to a spectacularly incorrect show called* The Black and White Minstrel Show, *which featured white singers blacked up. The point of this and the following small section might be lost in more enlightened times and locations, and can easily be substituted or omitted. But it should not be omitted on the grounds of offensiveness alone.*]

The song reaches a finale, then ends. Only then does **Stuart** *see the blacked-up male dancers.*

Stuart What the fuck is this?

Minstrel 1 What?

Stuart The blacking-up?

Minstrel 1 What about it?

Stuart What *about* it?

Minstrel 2 We're the Black and White Minstrels.

Stuart I know who you are. It's a bit fucking racist, isn't it?

Minstrel 3 It was your idea.

Stuart It wasn't *my* idea.

Minstrel 1 Whose idea was it then?

Minstrel 2 It wasn't fucking mine, that's for sure – I feel a right twat.

Minstrel 3 Me too.

Stuart It was whoever thought up *The Black and White Minstrels.*

Minstrel 1 Yeah, but you liked it.

Stuart I didn't like it – it was just on.

Pause.

Right, well, just – fuck off, the lot of you.

Minstrel 2 Don't fucking worry.

Minstrel 1 It *was* your idea.

They leave. **Stuart** *pulls his trousers down and sits on the toilet.*

Stuart It was just on.

Pause.

Yes, it was a big surprise to me. I'd always thought that you split up with someone because you'd stopped loving them, or realised you never did. But actually none of my relationships – my serious relationships – have ended that way. I've always loved them. There's been some other issue: a different outlook, a different dream; sometimes just practicalities. Nothing you wouldn't love someone for. Just things you can't live with peacefully. But I've felt the loss of every one of them, like a little death. It gets quite tiring after a while, the accumulation of losses.

He wipes his backside and looks at the toilet paper.

The accumulated losses. The accumulated losses of life.

Pause.

My next record? My next record is that one that's got the bit that goes 'I think I love you' that Angie used to play. If you're listening, Angie, please call. You said you'd fucking call.

[*Note: this is a reference to the radio programme* Desert Island Discs, *in which famous people choose their favourite records. In the original production, this scene ended with a repetitive sample of that one line 'I think I love you', taken from the song 'Take the Box' by Amy Winehouse, but this can be substituted. The point being that we often fixate on one line from a song. The sample then segued into a musical composition which served as the bridge between acts.*]

Music.

Above **Stuart**, *a shower unit comes on and he is sprayed with water as he sits there. He turns his face up to it, letting it clean him.*

Lights fade.

Act Two: Afternoon

[**Stuart** *washes his clothes. He is insulted by a telesales call.*]

Stuart, *now dressed, enters with a basket full of dirty washing.*

Stuart (*singing*)
What a bunch of cunts, what a bunch of cunts . . .

He opens the door of the washing machine and starts bundling the clothes in; but, from inside the machine, he hears his **Mother***'s voice:*

Mother (*muffled*) Have you checked the pockets?

Stuart What?

Mother (*muffled*) Have you looked in the pockets?

He removes some of the washing.

Stuart What are you saying?

Mother I said, have you checked the pockets of your trousers?

Stuart Yes . . .

Mother Are you sure?

Stuart There's nothing in the pockets.

Mother Because you know what happened to those tickets.

Stuart *sighs.*

Mother Why don't you check? Better safe than sorry.

Stuart (*exasperated*) Right, I'll check the fucking trousers.

Mother There's no need for language.

Stuart (*fondly*) There's no need for language.

He drags out a pair of trousers and checks the pockets. He finds something.

Mother What's that? Is that your bus pass?

Stuart No.

Mother So much for checking the pockets. Honestly, I think you'd –

Stuart *bundles the washing back in.*

Mother (*muffled*) – forget your own head if you didn't –

Stuart Yes, thank you, Mother.

He shuts the door. He empties powder into the tray, not sure how much to add. He sings a jingle from a washing-powder commercial:

'Washing machines live longer with Calgon.'

He crouches down to look at the settings.

What the fuck is a pre-wash? I never do a pre-wash. Maybe I should do a pre-wash?

Pause. He opens the door of the washing machine.

Mum – should I do a pre-wash?

A long pause. There is no answer. Of course not. He closes the door and turns the machine on. It trickles into life.

He looks in the basket. There's a sock in there.

Shit!

He tries to open the door but it's too late.

Exasperated, he takes the sock . . .

Right – you're going in the fucking bin!

. . . and throws it in the pedal bin.

He returns to the machine, watches it turn. The sound of the clothes sloshing.

Bored, he puts the basket on his head and clutches the slats as if they're the bars of a prison cell.

You've got to get me out of here!

This amuses him for a moment.

The sound of the machine gets louder and louder and more hypnotic. It reaches a crescendo and then stops.

The phone rings.

Stuart Hello?!

Salesman Is that Mr McWary?

Stuart Mr McQuarrie.

Salesman Oh, I beg your pardon – Mr McQuarrie: and can I just confirm with you that this is your home number?

Stuart Yes, obviously.

Salesman And is this a BT line, Mr McQuarrie?

Stuart Yes.

Salesman And if I was to tell you that you I could save you up to a hundred pounds a year on your phone bill, would that be of interest to you?

Stuart Em – not really, no.

Salesman I see. And what if I was to tell you that you could also enjoy over twenty extra channels of television at no extra cost – would that be of interest to you?

Stuart No, it wouldn't, but thanks – (for asking).

Salesman And you would also be able to enjoy free broadband at speeds of up to 8 MB depending on your area.

Stuart I'm sorry, but I'm really not interested. And I'm actually not that keen on being – (phoned at home).

Salesman Because all that can be yours with Teleport's Essentials package at an introductory price of just £13.99 a month for the first three months.

Stuart Right, well, you don't seem to be listening to me, but I'm really not interested, I'm sorry.

Pause.

Salesman You're not interested?

Stuart Sorry, no.

A pause, and then the **Salesman** *hangs up.*

Stuart Hello?

Nothing.

Fucking cheeky bastard!

Mullet *appears from under the bedding.*

Mullet You are one totally pathetic fucking loser!

Stuart What?

Mullet That guy just made an absolute cunt of you.

Stuart I know he did!

Mullet He made a fucking tit of you in your own house.

Stuart I know!

Mullet And you just let it happen.

Stuart Well, what was I supposed to do? I said I wasn't interested – I was trying to be polite.

Mullet Exactly. He basically said, 'I'm going to fuck you up the arse,' and you said, 'Yes, sir,' and spread your fat arse-cheeks.

Stuart Cheeky fucking bastard!

Mullet So what are you going to do about it?

The phone rings.

Stuart Hello?

Salesman Hello, is that Mr McWary?

Mullet *urges him on.*

Stuart If by Mr McWary you mean Mr McQuarrie, then yes.

Mullet *is disgusted with him.*

Salesman Oh, I beg your pardon – Mr McQuarrie: and can I just confirm with you that this is your – (home number)?

Mullet Is that it?

Stuart Eh?

Mullet 'If by Mr McWary you mean Mr McQuarrie' – is that all you're worried about? That he got your name wrong?

Stuart I was just starting.

Mullet You still said yes though, didn't you?

Stuart What am I supposed to say?

Mullet Tell the cunt to fuck off!

The phone rings.

Stuart Hello?

Salesman Hello, is that Mr McWary?

Stuart No, it fucking isn't!

Stuart *looks at* **Mullet**.

Salesman Oh – I'm sorry –

Mullet Tell him to fuck off!

Stuart Fuck off!

Pause. They seem pleased with themselves.

Salesman Hello?

Stuart He's still there!

Mullet Give it to the cunt!

Stuart Give him what?

Mullet It's a Saturday afternoon, for fuck's sake!

Stuart It's a Saturday afternoon, for fuck's sake!

Mullet *nods.*

Stuart Would you like me phoning you on a Saturday afternoon?

Pause.

No, I didn't think so; and I don't want any more shit TV channels so fuck off and don't call me again!

The phone hangs up.

That told him.

Mullet Yeah, but he still hung up on *you*. He's still got the power. He's phoned you up at your house, on your day off, and he's made you feel angry and bad.

Stuart What can I do about it?

Mullet Make *him* regret calling *you*. Spoil *his* fucking day!

Pause.

Stuart All right.

The phone rings.

Hello?

Salesman Hello, is that Mr McWary?

Stuart No, it's Mr McQuarrie.

Mullet *is annoyed with him. but* **Stuart** *indicates to wait.*

Salesman Oh, I beg your pardon – Mr McQuarrie. And could you just confirm that this is your home number?

Stuart Yes it is. But listen – are you calling from Teleport?

Pause.

Salesman Yes, I am.

Stuart Oh good, I was hoping you'd call.

Pause.

Salesman Were you?

Stuart Yes, and listen, I'm very interested in your product but would you mind calling back in about ten minutes? It's just that I'm wanking at the moment.

Salesman I'm sorry?

Stuart I said I'm wanking at the moment – but I should have come in about five minutes so if you could call back then, that'd be perfect.

Mullet *is delighted.*

Salesman Oh – right . . .

Stuart I mean, unless you'd like to stay on the line and talk me through it, you know – say something like, 'Ooh yes, ooh yes, wank it,' over and over again. Would that interest you at all, you little fucking maggot?

Pause.

I'm asking you a question, you subhuman piece of shit – would that interest you?

Salesman No, sir – it wouldn't.

Stuart Right – well, then, *you* can fuck off!

The phone goes dead. They are triumphant. They run around whooping in triumph.

Mullet That was fucking great!

Stuart He'll think twice about doing that again.

Mullet God, you were quite vicious there. 'Subhuman piece of shit'?

Stuart Well, I'll take abuse up to a certain point –

Mullet Yeah, but there's a line.

Stuart But there's a line, and if you cross it – doesn't matter who you are –

Mother Stuart!

They both jump out of their skins.

Mother Stuart McQuarrie! What do you think you're playing at?!

Stuart What?

Mother Don't 'what' me! I heard the filth you were saying! What was the meaning of it?

Stuart I didn't start it.

Mother Who did then?

Stuart The guy on the phone – he called me up, out of the blue –

Mother I know what he did. I don't remember him saying any filth to you.

Stuart No, well, he didn't; but when I said I wasn't interested, he just hung up on me. Which was pretty bloody rude.

She slaps him round the head.

Mother There's no need for language!

Stuart You shouldn't hit people on the head, it gives them brain damage.

Mother I'll brain damage you.

Pause.

So he hung up on you. Which was rude . . .

Stuart So I decided to be rude back.

Mother Oh, the Big Man, is it? The Head Cheese.

Mullet *smirks.*

Mother Making someone feel small over the phone.

Stuart He hung up on me.

Mother Did he? Are you sure that's what happened? Let's ask him, shall we?

Stuart Ask him?

Mother Yes – because he's here. Simon?!

She looks offstage.

Come and give him a hand.

Stuart *and* **Mullet** *look at* **Simon** *– who we cannot yet see – and then at each other.*

Mother Come on then.

She nods them in an offstage direction. **Stuart** *makes* **Mullet** *accompany him. They exit.*

Muffled sounds of effort offstage.

They return with **Simon**. *He's in a wheelchair, attached to an IV drip.* **Mother** *helps bring him onstage. One of* **Simon***'s arms is tiny and malformed.*

Mother Simon, this – I'm ashamed to say – is my son. Stuart – this is the man you called subhuman.

Simon Hello.

He extends his small hand. **Stuart** *and* **Mullet** *shake it.*

Stuart Hello.

Mullet Hi.

Simultaneously:

Simon Why don't you –

Mother Listen, I just –

Simon Sorry –

Mother No, you go ahead.

Simon I just wanted to say that it's really all right. I completely understand – we get enough adverts thrown at us without people calling you up at home and trying to sell things. Believe me, I feel embarrassed every time I call someone. It's just that, obviously, given my condition, you know – playing for England was never an option.

Stuart Oh, I don't know . . .

Mother Stuart!

Stuart Oh well, look – I'm sorry that you're disabled and all that and obviously I feel a bit bad. But it doesn't change the fact that as soon as I said I wasn't interested, you just hung up on me; and that's just rude, whatever . . . condition you're in.

Mother Oh, and you're such a big know-it-all, aren't you? The Big I-Am. Well, tell him, Simon.

Simon Oh really, it's all right. He wasn't to know.

Pause.

Stuart Wasn't to know what?

Mother It just so happens, Mr Smarty-Pants, that Simon didn't hang up on you; he actually had a seizure.

Pause.

Simon I felt it coming on during the conversation. I'd have said goodbye but my jaw sort of locks, so I can't speak.

Pause.

Mother Thank you, Simon.

Pause.

I hope you're proud of yourself, Stuart McQuarrie. Maybe you'll not be so quick to judge in future.

She wheels him offstage.

Stuart *and* **Mullet** *are left there, in their shame.*

The sound of the washing machine turning.

Mullet *sits by it and puts the basket on his head, as* **Stuart** *had earlier.*

Stuart *makes his way back to the couch.*

Pause.

The **Cat** *ambles slowly in.*

Stuart Ah, here he is. Where have you been all night? Chasing all the girl cats I bet.

Cat Fuck you.

The **Cat** *walks straight to the bowl of cat food and smells it.*

Cat Muck.

And with this, he turns and walks slowly out again.

Stuart *tries to stroke him as he passes, but the* **Cat** *shrugs him off.*

Angie *enters. She's trying on clothes for an evening out.*

Angie What's wrong with Galloway?

Stuart He's spoiled.

Angie Well, if he's spoiled it's because you spoiled him.

Stuart I don't spoil him. They must have been feeding him salmon or something.

Angie At a rescue centre? I doubt it. Anyway, don't change the subject.

Stuart What was the subject?

Angie You being a homophobe.

Pause.

Pleading the Fifth, I see.

Stuart I don't care if you think I'm a homophobe. I know I'm not.

Angie But being gay revolts you?

Stuart I didn't say being *gay* revolts me.

Angie What did you say then?

Stuart I don't care if people are gay. I'm actually in favour of it.

Angie Why, because it narrows the competition?

Stuart Exactly. And they're all the best-looking guys as well. Everybody wins.

Angie You said it revolts you.

Stuart No, I said that if you're a heterosexual man – regardless of how enlightened you are – you find the thought of, you know –

Angie What?

Stuart The thought of coming into direct contact with another man's . . .

Angie Cock.

Stuart Yes –

Angie You can't even say it.

Stuart Can't even say what?

Angie Another man's cock.

Stuart Another man's cock.

Angie There, you see? Still heterosexual.

She kisses him.

Stuart You are so fucking annoying, d'you know that?

Angie And you're a homophobe.

Pause.

And a racist.

Stuart How am I a fucking racist now?!

Angie Cos every time you tell me what Mr Rajah's said you put on that stupid accent.

Stuart That's not being racist.

Angie It is so . . . 'All reduced – Mr Rajah's all reduced!'

Stuart That's how he talks!

Angie You don't have to do the wee shake of the head.

Stuart So *The Simpsons* is racist, is it?

Angie Yes.

Pause.

Stuart I'm not a fucking racist. There's not a racist bone in my body. In fact I go out of my way to not be racist.

Angie How?

Stuart Well – if an Asian shopkeeper –

Angie 'An Asian shopkeeper – '

Stuart Yes – if an Asian shopkeeper gives me change, I always make a point of just making slight contact with his hand.

Angie What's that supposed to prove?

Stuart Well, you know – just to make sure he knows I don't think I'll get the Paki touch or something. And – if I get on a bus, and there's an Asian person sitting there –

Angie Don't tell me – you sit beside them.

Stuart Yes! Even if there are other seats!

Angie You are such a fucking wanker, Stuart McQuarrie.

Stuart Ah, but who's more of a wanker? The wanker, or the wanker that loves the wanker?

Angie *pushes him away.*

Angie I don't love you.

Pause.

You love me.

Stuart Yes. I do.

He embraces her. Pause.

Angie D'you want to shag?

Pause. He looks at his watch.

Stuart Yeah, all right.

She pulls him down behind the couch. We hear their voices, as they struggle off with their clothes.

Stuart Can you bum your girlfriend?

Angie Can I bum my girlfriend?

Stuart Can *one* bum one's girlfriend? I mean – you hear about men bumming each other but you never hear someone say, 'I bummed my girlfriend.'

Angie I'll fucking bum you.

Stuart You'll bum me?

Angie Will you shut the fuck up?!

We hear the sound of them starting to make love.

Father *enters and stops as he sees them.*

Father What's going on here?!

Suddenly, from behind the couch, up spring **Stuart** *and* **Laura**, *looking flustered.*

Mullet *suddenly springs into life.*

Mullet Stewpot, look! Porno!

He waves a tatty old porno mag that he's found.

Stuart Not now!

Laura *runs out, distressed, clutching her blouse to her chest.*

Stuart *half follows her.*

Stuart Laura!

Mullet *finds more pornography in the sand.*

Mullet There's more, look! It's like treasure!

Angie *appears from behind the couch.*

Angie You dirty bastard!

She storms out.

Stuart Angie – it's not mine!

Mullet Look at this!

Stuart *runs to* **Mullet**.

Stuart I can't just now.

Mullet But look at the fanny on that!

Stuart Christ.

Mother (*enters*) Stuart!

Stuart I've got to go

Mullet Later, then.

Stuart Yeah, later.

Mother Stuart, get over here now!

Stuart *runs back and sits on the couch, shamefaced.*

Father Well, I think we have to tell them.

Mother Oh, shut your silly mouth. We don't have to tell anyone anything.

Father If it was the other way round, we'd want to know.

Mother Have you met Laura's parents?

Father No, but – (that's not the point).

Mother Then shut your silly mouth, you old jessie.

Father Don't call me a jessie, Margaret. Not in front of Stuart.

Mother (*mimics*) 'Don't call me a jessie, don't call me a jessie.'

Father Right, well, you sort it out then; because I give up, I just bloody give up!

He walks out.

Mother 'I just bloody give up.'

Stuart *and his* **Mother** *share a conspiratorial laugh.*

Pause.

Mother So – what are we going to do with the two of you?

Pause. **Stuart** *shrugs.*

Mother He may be an old jessie, but you know what they say, even a stopped clock's right twice a day. When we've got Laura under our roof, we've got a duty of care. We've got a responsibility, to make sure she doesn't get up to anything that her parents wouldn't want her getting up to. You know what Jesus said: 'Suffer the little children.'

Stuart *looks confused.*

Mother What do you think of her?

She pokes at him.

Stuart. Stuart.

Stuart Who?!

Mother Don't act the daft laddie. What do you think of Laura?

Pause.

Do you love her?

Pause. He shrugs uncomfortably.

Just a shrug.

Stuart Aw, Mum!

Mother Don't 'Aw, Mum' me, it's important. You put your swizzle-stick inside a girl and babies are what's next.

Stuart *groans and puts a cushion over his head.*

Mother Now don't be such a baby. It's a thing for a girl that age to have a child. She's just a little thing too. She's not got a big fat bum and hips like me. A baby'd rip her from front to back.

Stuart *groans. She prises the cushion away from him.*

Mother Listen to me, Stuart. You know what Jesus said: 'Respect your mother.'

Stuart He never said that!

Mother You weren't there, you don't know. Now listen to me: do you get all excited when you think of her? And I don't mean your swizzle-stick –

Stuart Stop saying that!

Mother I mean, down your back, a little shiver. And do you want to say her name over and over? Do you find excuses to say it? Laura Laura Laura!

She teases him.

And do you hug the pillow and pretend it's her?

He throws the cushion aside.

Stuart No!

Mother Ah, you see – a picture tells a hundred tales.

Pause.

And is it like all the other girls just disappear? Like they don't exist? Like she's the only girl in the world?

(*Sings.*)
'If you were the only girl in the world,
And I was the only boy . . . '

She smiles. Pause.

Well, you listen to me –

He covers his ears. She wrenches the cushion away, so seriously it startles him.

I'm being serious, Stuart, this is important!

Pause.

Don't you pay any mind to what anyone says. There's nothing worse you can do in this world than marry for the sake of appearance. If you feel all those things about a girl, then maybe she's the one. But if you don't, or if you think you might not feel them ten years down the line, then you let her go, no matter how she cries; and do it sooner, not later. Let her be free to find someone who does feel that. You be alone rather than that; rather than fight like cat and dog all your life; rather than die a bit at a time. That's what a real man does for a woman. That's what he does for himself.

Pause.

Don't you settle for less than love, than true love, do you hear me? Don't you settle for less!

Pause.

Laura *enters.*

Mother Here she is.

Laura *sits on the couch with* **Stuart**.

Mother You feeling better?

Laura *nods.*

Laura I like your mirror.

Mother Which?

Laura The big one in the hall.

Mother That was my mother's. Yes.

Pause.

My mother gave that to me.

Classical music plays, and **Stuart** *lies down to listen to it. With one hand, he half conducts.*

Mother, *bare-footed and parasol in hand, walks across the sand.*

[*Note: in the original production, this next scene played out as if on a beach, but the location, in itself, is unimportant and you may wish to change it depending on your stage design.*]

Mother *walks around a rock pool. She stares up at the sun.*

Suddenly she becomes unsteady on her feet, totters slightly, and then collapses, face down.

Bystander 1, *who has been talking on his mobile phone, runs to her. He crouches down beside her, unsure what to do.*

Bystander 2 *rushes in, having seen the collapse.*

Bystander 1 *calls for an ambulance.*

Seeing a coastguard, **Bystander 2** *rushes offstage towards him.*

Father *enters, in holiday clothes, carrying a bag of shopping. When he sees his wife collapsed, he drops his shopping and runs to her, but it is too late.*

He cradles her in his arms.

Bystander 2 *returns. Lights fade on this tableau. The music ends. The washing machine churns to a halt.*

Act Three: Night

[**Stuart** *has something to eat. He watches television. He goes to bed.*]

Stuart *looks at his watch.*

He gets up and goes to the fridge, opens it.

He takes out a ready meal.

Laura *enters.*

Laura Oh Stuart!

Stuart What?

Laura What's that?

Stuart It's a prawn curry thing.

Laura *is disapproving.*

Stuart What?

Laura I'll bet it's full of E-numbers.

Stuart What's wrong with E-numbers?

Laura They're bad for you.

Stuart Everything's bad for you.

Stuart *pierces the film, puts the meal in the microwave and starts it cooking.*

Laura You shouldn't use microwaves either. They make you infertile.

Stuart Good. Won't have to bother with johnnies.

Laura Don't say good. What if we want to have children?

Stuart Laura, for fuck's sake – will you get off my back? If you want to go out with a leaf-eating, non-smoking, rice-eating wank then do it. But stop trying to turn me into one.

Pause.

Laura I'm just saying it because I don't want you to die.

Stuart Awww.

Laura Who'll look after all the animals if you die?

Stuart Oh I don't *know* . . .

Laura Oh, oh – I've thought of another one! Koala bears! We've got to have some koala bears!

Stuart Aren't they vicious?

Laura Koala bears? They're lovely!

Stuart I stand corrected.

Laura But we'll have to grow eucalyptus trees because that's all they eat.

Stuart Yeah, well – we're growing bamboo for the pandas anyway.

Laura I think we'll have to build another biosphere, just for plants.

Stuart This started out as a small farmhouse in France and now it's like Blofeld's fucking secret complex. Who's going to pay for all this?

Laura I am!

Stuart You are? Because it's going to cost about a billion pounds.

Laura Yeah, well, it's a dream house. You can't put a price on a dream house!

She exits.

Stuart You can't put a price on a dream house . . .

The microwave pings.

Stuart *takes out the meal. He peels back the film, stirs it, then places it back inside.*

He sits on the couch. Only the light from the TV on his face, which is fixed in an inane grin. A high-pitched noise sounds.

The doorbell rings. Lights up again. **Stuart** *looks puzzled.*

The doorbell rings again. He gets up to answer it, leaving the stage.

The light bulbs sway. A breeze shifts the sand. Pause.

Paul *enters, carrying a bag.* **Stuart** *is displeased.*

Paul I know, I know – you said you were doing nothing.

Stuart Yeah, and I sort of meant it.

Paul Yeah, well, there was nothing going on at the Duck. Fucking girlfriends, I'm telling you – they're ruining the world. D'you want to stick these in the fridge?

He hands him some cans of beer. **Stuart** *groans.*

Paul We don't have to drink them all. We'll just have a beer and see how it goes; if you still 'vant to be alone', I'll piss off – Scout's honour.

Stuart *puts them in the fridge.*

Paul *sits on the couch. He unwraps some food.*

Paul I got you some chips.

Stuart I just put something in the microwave.

Paul What?

Stuart A prawn curry.

Paul That'll go with chips. What's this? *Millionaire*?

He opens a can of beer and hands one to **Stuart**, *then opens one for himself. They fill their glasses.*

Paul Look at this cunt. He's used a lifeline already and he's not even up to five hundred.

Stuart, *resigned to his fate, sits on the couch beside him.*

Paul D – Jon Pertwee.

Again only the TV light plays on their faces. They stare at the television, with those same inane grins. The same whining sound. It suddenly ends and they return to normality.

Paul That was shite. It's about time they put that to bed. What's on the other side?

Stuart Let's just see the headlines.

Again – the light, the grins, the sound. Lights up.

Paul The Israelis are a deeply misunderstood people.

Stuart Fuck . . .

Paul What?

Stuart I had a dream . . . something to do with Israel . . .

Paul What's this?

Once more – the lights, the sound. but only **Stuart** *is grinning.* **Paul** *immediately falls asleep. Lights up.* **Paul** *wakes.*

Paul Who did it?

Stuart The guy with the haircut.

Paul His mate?

Stuart Yeah.

Paul Told you. Shall we partake of another 'tinnie'?

Stuart Yeah, go on.

Paul On you go then.

Stuart Me?

Paul You're the host.

Stuart Didn't get much choice in the matter, did I?

Pause. He sighs.

These are nice chips.

He gets up to go to the fridge. **Paul** *watches him intently.*

Stuart Fuck . . .

Pause.

Paul What is it?

Pause.

Stuart I feel really funny.

Pause.

Fuck . . .

He drops to his knees. The chips spill out of his hand across the floor.

Paul, I'm not joking – something's really wrong . . .

He rolls on to his back. **Paul** *gets up to look at him.*

Stuart Call – an ambulance –

Paul Can you move?

Stuart No –

Paul Try and move your hand.

Pause. Nothing.

Stuart Oh Jesus – what's happening to me?

Pause. **Paul** *looks around. He takes a cushion from the couch.*

He squats down beside **Stuart**.

Stuart Paul –

Paul Have you got anything to say?

Stuart *can barely even make a sound.*

Paul Stuart – look at me; have you got anything to say – you *cunt*.

Pause. With great effort:

Stuart Tell Angie – that I love her. Tell her – I don't know – why I left her – like I did.

Pause. **Paul** *nods.*

He places the cushion over **Stuart**'*s face.*

We hear his muffled shouts for a while, then they fade.

After a while, **Paul** *removes the cushion.*

Breathing heavily, **Paul** *stares down at* **Stuart**'*s corpse.*

The doorbell rings, startling him.

For a moment he doesn't know what to do.

The doorbell rings again.

Paul There in a minute!

With great effort, he drags **Stuart**'*s body out of sight.*

Mullet *appears, peering over the back of the couch, watching this.*

The doorbell rings again.

Paul *enters, out of breath.*

Paul Just a moment!

And then he sees **Mullet**. *Their eyes meet.* **Paul** *puts his finger to his mouth – 'Shhhhh.'*

Paul *straightens himself up and goes to answer the door.*

The light bulbs sway.

Voices offstage.

Paul Angie, hi.

Angie Hi, Paul. Is Stuart here?

They enter.

Paul Eh – he's not, actually.

Angie Where is he?

Paul I don't know. Is he not with you?

Angie No, why? Did he say he was seeing me?

Paul I think so . . .

Angie No. I was meant to give him a call but I wasn't seeing him. Not as far as I know.

Paul Oh right. I thought that was what he said.

She looks around the flat. **Paul**, *nervous, positions himself in front of where he dragged* **Stuart**'*s body.*

Angie What are you doing here?

Paul Do you want a beer or something?

Angie No, I'm all right.

Pause.

What are you doing here?

Paul We were down the Duck's Arse, you know – earlier. Had a couple of pints and then we were coming back here, but he had to do something – I thought he said he was seeing you, or calling you or something. So he said for me to wait here. I thought that was him.

She nods, obviously suspicious.

Angie When was this?

Paul Eight or so. I mean, I tried phoning him but . . .

Their talk fades, to be replaced by music. This is what we would hear them saying (or as much as you need for the moment).

Paul . . . it always seems to be busy. I don't know, I just assumed maybe he was on the phone to you. To be honest I assumed you were maybe having a bit of a barney. Sorry, but you know how it is. Best not to interfere with these things. So, you know – I just made myself comfortable here, had a few beers, watched the TV, that sort of thing. But I am getting a wee bit worried. It's been a couple of hours now and if he wasn't seeing you, then I don't know who he could have been seeing. It isn't really like him whichever way you look at it.

Angie No it's not.

Paul I don't know – what do you think we should do? Maybe we should go out looking for him. I'm sure there's some explanation for it. Maybe he met someone. We could always try the Duck, maybe he's gone back there. I did sort of foist myself on him. Maybe he had some other plans that he didn't want to tell me about.

But instead . . .

A spotlight – signifying **Angie***'s point of view – moves across the floor, highlighting: the two glasses of beer, the two cans, the spilled chips and then the tracks left in the sand by* **Stuart***'s dragged body. The spotlight follows the tracks off into the wings.*

Mullet *still watches, silently, from behind the couch.*

The sound returns.

Paul No, I'm sure there's an explanation for it.

Pause.

Angie (*scared*) I'll try phoning him.

Paul I've tried him a few times. There's no answer.

Pause.

Angie Can't hurt to try again.

Pause.

Paul Tell you what – let's try down the Duck. We can give him a call on the way.

He puts his jacket on. Pause.

Angie All right.

They exit. **Angie** *casts a look backwards as she leaves.*

Pause. The sand shifts again.

A mobile phone rings: the ringtone is reminiscent of the ice-cream van heard earlier.

Mullet *slowly appears from behind the couch. He sits down cross-legged and starts eating the chips from the floor.*

Music.

From everywhere come the mourners, all moving slowly.

Laura *looks like a grieving supermodel, her movements strangely jerky as she walks to position.*

Stuart*'s* **Father** *enters slowly, in a black suit.*

Stuart*'s* **Mother***, all in white, descends from the ceiling to come to a stop only feet above the ground.*

The **Cat***, Galloway, enters, dragging a dead bird.*

They take their positions around the room, forming a bizarre tableau.

The music ends.

Mother I remember one winter, it had just snowed – this was back when it snowed in winter – I looked out of the window of our house, down into the square, and I saw him in his little school uniform –

Father He could never keep his shirt-tails in, could he?

Mother No, that's right. Or his laces done up. But anyway, I looked down and – before he came into the stair – I saw him deliberately rolling in the snow, you know; getting it all over himself. So I'd make a fuss of him when he came in. Give him a nice bowl of home-made soup. I think that was the only thing I cooked that he actually liked.

Pause.

Laura Yeah, cos I remember when it was snowing; and I think we'd had a bit of an argument. No, I think we'd actually split up; yeah, that's right. And we both spent about a week in misery but not knowing if the other one was bothered. And then one morning I came out of my mum's house to go to school and all this snow had fallen and it was all untouched; except outside my door, and on all the cars, and everywhere, someone had written 'I love you Laura'. Everywhere you could see.

Mother Stuart?

Laura He must've got up really early and come over to my house and done it all before I got up.

Mother He did love you, Laura. I know you had your ups and downs; but he really did. And you, Angie. But I think you've always got a soft spot for the first.

Angie *shrugs, absorbing the veiled insult.*

Father Well, that must've been the only time he ever got up early. D'you remember – he got into terrible trouble for being late at school?

Mother Oh dear, yes. What a palaver that was. They had us in, didn't they?

Father They were going to expel him!

Mother That's right, they were.

Father They were going to expel him if he was late just once more. So he came up with this foolproof system – he put a bucket of cold water by his bed. The theory being, when his alarm clock went off, rather than just turning it off and going back to sleep as usual, he would immediately plunge his whole head into this bucket of water. Well – come the morning – off goes the alarm, Stuart bolts awake, rolls over – takes one look at the water, says, 'Not a chance,' and just goes back to sleep again!

Laughter.

Angie If he had to leave before me in the morning, he'd always put one of my teddy bears in bed beside me, with its little arm over me.

Affectionate nodding. Pause.

Mother Galloway – you must have a few stories about Stuart?

Pause. Galloway considers it.

Cat He was a prick.

Pause. **Father** *raises his glass.*

Father To Stuart.

They raise their glasses.

All To Stuart.

Music.

Stuart *appears now. They all turn to see him.*

They begin to clap. They applaud him as he walks down to them, his arms open, almost messianic.

He kisses **Angie**.

He shakes his **Father***'s hand and tries, awkwardly, to hug him.*

He hugs his **Mother** *tight.*

He attempts to stroke Galloway, but the **Cat** *swipes him with his claws.*

He high-fives **Mullet**.

Finally, he embraces **Laura**.

Laura *and* **Angie** *remove his clothes until he is as he was at the beginning of the play.*

His **Father** *and* **Mother** *prepare his bed.*

The **Cat** *picks up the dead bird and leaves.*

Stuart *is led up to the bed. His* **Father** *tucks him under the covers. His* **Mother** *kisses his forehead. They exit.*

Mullet *takes one last look at his friend, peaceful in bed now, then leaves.*

The bed slowly lifts up to a vertical position. Over this:

Stuart (*on tape*)
And now I lay me down to sleep
I pray the Lord my soul to keep
And if I die before I wake
I pray my soul the Lord to take.

Stuart *sleeps, as if we are looking down on him.*

The phone rings. He wakes and answers it. **Angie** *is voice only.*

Stuart Hello?

Angie Stuart? It's Angie. Did I wake you?

Stuart Eh – no, no.

Angie Are you in bed?

Stuart Yeah, but I'm awake. I thought you were going to call me.

Angie I am calling you.

Stuart I thought you were going to call me earlier.

Pause.

Angie You wanted to speak to me.

Stuart Yes, of course –

Pause.

Angie I don't care about my things. Throw them away if you want.

Pause.

Stuart That's not what I wanted to say . . .

Angie What then?

Stuart Is it a bad time?

Angie A bad time?

Stuart You seem in a hurry.

Angie It's late.

Stuart Whose fault is that?

Angie Don't start or I'll hang up.

Stuart Don't hang up.

Angie Then say what you've got to say.

Pause.

Stuart Jesus, Angie – does it have to be like this?

Angie Like what?

Stuart Look – I know you won't believe me, Angie. But I love you. I really do.

Pause.

Angie Stuart . . .

Stuart And I know, so why did I finish it? But you've got to believe me when I say – I don't know. I truly don't know. There was no reason for it; I'm not seeing anyone else, I wasn't unhappy. I didn't do it because of what's happening now. I did it because – of what would happen in the future.

Pause.

Angie Why are you telling me this?

Stuart Because I don't want to live without you.

Pause.

Angie What does that mean?

Stuart It means what it means. It means that I love you. That's a precious thing. Do you know how precious that is?

Pause.

I know you're hurt. But let's not throw everything away.

Angie You're really confusing me.

Pause.

What are you saying? Are you saying you regret it – what?

Long pause.

Stuart No. I'm not saying I regret it. I think it was the right thing to do, for both of our sakes. But I didn't do it because I don't love you.

Pause.

Why don't we meet up?

Angie No.

Stuart Why not?

Angie You know why not.

Pause.

It's over, Stuart. It has to be.

Pause.

Stuart We can't even be friends?

Angie I don't know. Not now.

Stuart But some day.

Angie I don't know. Maybe – who knows? But for now – stop calling me. Please. Please, Stuart.

Pause.

I have to go now.

Stuart Not like this.

Angie What do you mean?

Stuart I mean let's not make it a big goodbye. I can't handle it, not just now.

Pause.

Just talk to me for a while. Talk to me like we'll be seeing each other tomorrow.

Pause.

Angie What do you want me to say?

Stuart I don't know. Anything.

Pause.

Angie How's Galloway?

Stuart He's fine. Surly, as usual.

Pause.

Angie What did you do today?

Stuart Today?

Pause.

Fuck all.

The lights by now have faded to black.

Epilogue

[*In the original production, the following happened. Obviously, it was an expensive sequence but I shall go on to explain the element of it that should be preserved.*]

A box is flown in.

When the lights come up, it is revealed as a kitchen. The furniture – the washing machine, the cooker, the fridge etc. – is exactly the same as that which is dotted around the set, but is now in its proper place. It looks very real.

A door opens and **Stuart** *enters. He then proceeds – in real time and with no fuss – to make himself a cup of tea. This done, he sits at the kitchen table.*

He drinks his tea.

The lights come up. Slowly, the audience realises it is expected to leave. **Stuart** *continues drinking his tea, lost in his thoughts.*

Eventually, the theatre empties.

[*Note: in previous versions, I have suggested this ending is optional, but now I feel it should be preserved. For those with limited resources, all that is necessary is that we see Stuart – the next morning – making a cup of tea, in real time, and sitting down quietly to drink it. Let the audience sit with this image for some time before bringing the lights down. The interior of Stuart's mind is now closed to them. A curtain call may now be taken for those who bristle at the thought of denying the audience (and the actors) some finality.*]